goose

ALSO BY MELANIE DENNIS UNRAU

Nonfiction

The Rough Poets: Reading Oil-Worker Poetry

Poetry

Happiness Threads: The Unborn Poems

PRAISE FOR *GOOSE*

"*Goose* is a masterful work of reinterpretation, revealing brilliant strands of critique and resistance within the romanticized poems and drawings of the self-styled 'father of the tar sands.' Language, image, land, and labouring bodies break free of Sidney Ells's narrow preconceptions here, unravelling the colonial logic of extractive industry and presenting instead a vibrant, nuanced way of understanding energy and belonging."

—Warren Cariou, author of *Lake of the Prairies*

"Honk if you're ready to ruffle the colonial archive! *Goose* is one of those rare and wonderful works that just sits beautifully, irreverently, and wholly in its hybridity, its experimentation, and its genre-bending, and never once tries to justify itself. In this sharp, witty, funny, and deeply political collection, Melanie Dennis Unrau raises a delicately inked middle finger to extractivist nostalgia. Tracing and transforming the settler boosterism of Sidney Clarke Ells, she reclaims the page with each gestural mark and cheeky erasure. The result is, like every goose, fierce, silly, and totally ungovernable."

—Dani Spinosa, author of *OO: Typewriter Poems*

"*Goose* is far more than experimental poetry: it is call and response, disintegration and repair. These poems cast a long, hard look at S. C. Ells's contributions, as 'the father of the tar sands,' to the colonial prosperity of Alberta and the ecological devastation that followed in his and others' footsteps. The collection speaks from within the stacks of the archives and the living tissue of community stories; ebullient and interrogatory, these poems sound their presence as clearly as the geese."

—Jenna Butler, author of *Revery: A Year of Bees*

goose

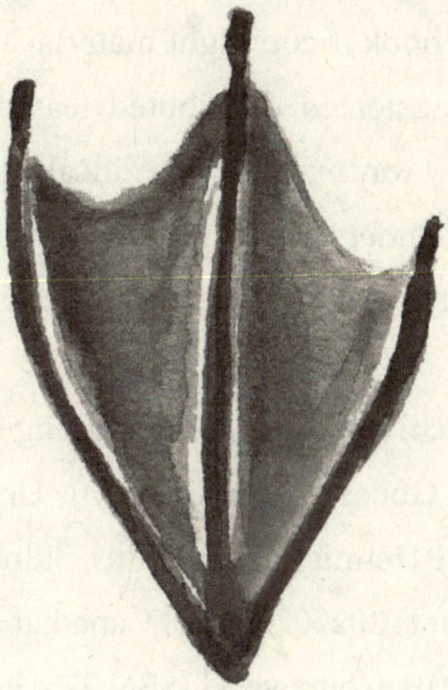

MELANIE DENNIS UNRAU

Assembly Press
Prince Edward County, Ontario

Library and Archives Canada Cataloguing in Publication
Title: Goose / Melanie Dennis Unrau.
Names: Unrau, Melanie Dennis, author. | Ells, Sidney Clarke, 1879-1971.
Identifiers: Canadiana (print) 20250235137 | Canadiana (ebook) 2025023761X | ISBN 9781998336210 (softcover) | ISBN 9781998336227 (EPUB)
Subjects: LCGFT: Visual poetry. | LCGFT: Found poetry. | LCGFT: Poetry.
Classification: LCC PS8641.N744 G66 2025 | DDC C811/.6—dc23

Published by Assembly Press | assemblypress.ca
Cover and interior designed by Greg Tabor

Printed and bound in Canada on uncoated paper made from 100% recycled content in line with our commitment to ethical business practices and sustainability.

for the trackers

TABLE OF CONTENTS

FOREWORD

There is a long history in Canada and indeed across the world of European "explorers" appropriating the knowledge, skills, and labour of Indigenous peoples for their personal and collective gain, only to turn around and declare the territories of Indigenous peoples "terra nullius," and their cultures and ways of live inferior and unworthy of respect. This dialectic of appropriation-negation is familiar to Indigenous peoples across the globe. And so it is with Fort McMurray, its oil sands, and their "father," Sidney Ells. Through research, community and public awareness, and the construction of our cultural centre, McMurray Métis hope to correct these self-serving and distorted narratives, and assert our historic and continued presence, way of life, and self-determination. Let this foreword be one small step in that direction.

The history of Fort McMurray is a Métis history. Our ancestors came to Fort McMurray via La Loche, Lac La Biche, and Athabasca Landing. They built ingenious ships, including skiffs and scows, that could transport goods across the treacherous rapids of the Athabasca River then be taken apart and used to construct homes in the north. The famous captains of the era—Fosseneuve, Bird, McDonald, Loutitt, and more—are among our Métis forefathers who taught us to navigate the waters. Our ancestors who towed the boats and hauled the furs—known as "trackers"—taught us the value and pride of hard work. Together, our ancestors built homes in Fort

McMurray and on river lots of the Athabasca, trapped in the winters, and built the early industries of Fort McMurray, from logging and salt to fisheries. They lived in harmony with the lands and waters that sustained our unique way of life and culture, balancing our traditional harvesting and stewardship of our lands and waters with the commercial opportunities opened up by Euro-Canadian expansion.

When steamships, tugboats, and eventually railroads replaced skiffs and scows, our ancestors captained the ships, cut cord to fuel the boats, and worked the docks and rails. We built the first school and settled our families in Fort McMurray, a small Indigenous town of 1,100 people until the second half of the 1960s. When the era of large-scale oil-sands operations began, our people helped to build the early industry. But something changed: the balance of our way of life was undermined by the large-scale destruction of our lands and waters. Our people were dispossessed by the influx of tens of thousands of Euro-Canadian settlers, and our history was buried under the triumphant narrative of technological and economic "progress."

McMurray Métis was established as the governance arm of the Métis community of Fort McMurray in response to the onslaught of oil-sands development in the 1960s and 1970s that transformed our small Indigenous town into one of Canada's centres of resource and wealth extraction. Today, McMurray Métis is committed to reclaiming Fort McMurray as a Métis space, in which the history, adaptation, transmission, and thriving of our way of life and culture is supported. We have rebuilt our traditional scows. We have created our Métis Trackers program, which teaches our youth the pride of labour in the service of community. We offer courses and programs to teach our cultural and artistic forms. And we are building our McMurray Métis Cultural Centre on MacDonald Island, settled by the McDonald family from Red River in 1870, which was taken from our people in the dispossessions of the 1960s and 1970s.

We invite you to explore the rich and complex history of our people and of Fort McMurray, through dissections of colonial sources like you will find in this book, by exploring Indigenous histories and sources, and by visiting us here in Fort McMurray. *Tânsi*. We look forward to meeting you.

McMurray Métis

The Goose

geese

geese

geese

geese

geese

geese

geese

goose geese

geese

goose goose

geese

geese

geese

geese

geese

geese

geese

geese

geese goose

geese
geese
geese
geese
geese and ducks
geese

geese
ducks
goose geese
geese
goose goose
geese

geese
geese
geese
geese and
ducks

geese
geese
geese
geese goose

geese geese

geese

geesegeese

geese

geese geese

geese

goose

geese

geese geese

geese

geese geese

geese

geese

goose

geese

geese

geese

geese

goose

geese geese

goose

geese goose goose

geese

geese

geese

geesegeese and ducks

ducks

geese

geese geese

geese

goose

geese

geese

geese

geese

geese

geese

geese

geese

goose

geese

geese

geese and ducks

geese

goose

geese

geese

goose

goose

geese

goose

geese geese

geese

geesegeese ducks

hosts of

wild ducks

geese

geese

geese

geese

goose

geese

geese geese

geese

geese

Hosts of geese

geese

hosts of geese

goose

hosts of geese

geese

geese and ducks

birds

waterfowl waterfowl

geese

goose

hosts

hosts of geese *geese*

geese goose goose

goose

Grey geese
south-bound geese
wild geese

Wild geese

grey
weary

geese
Grey geese
grey geese
geese

grey goose
geese

gray geese
geese

geese

geese
southbound geese
grey geese

grey geese

marshalled
geese
gray goose
grey geese

geese

geese
gray
goose

grey geese
weary geese

Grey geese
gray goose
gray goose
grey goose

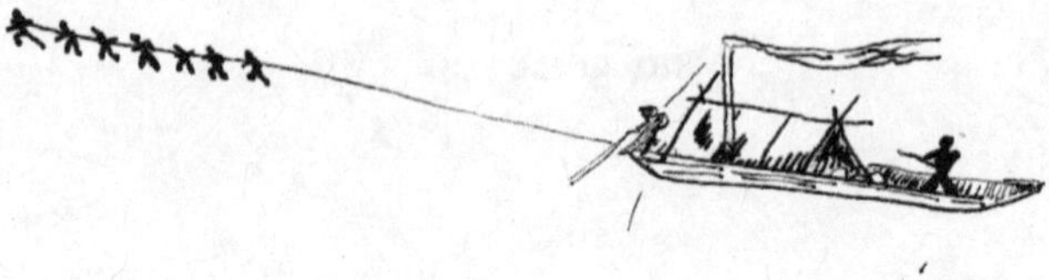

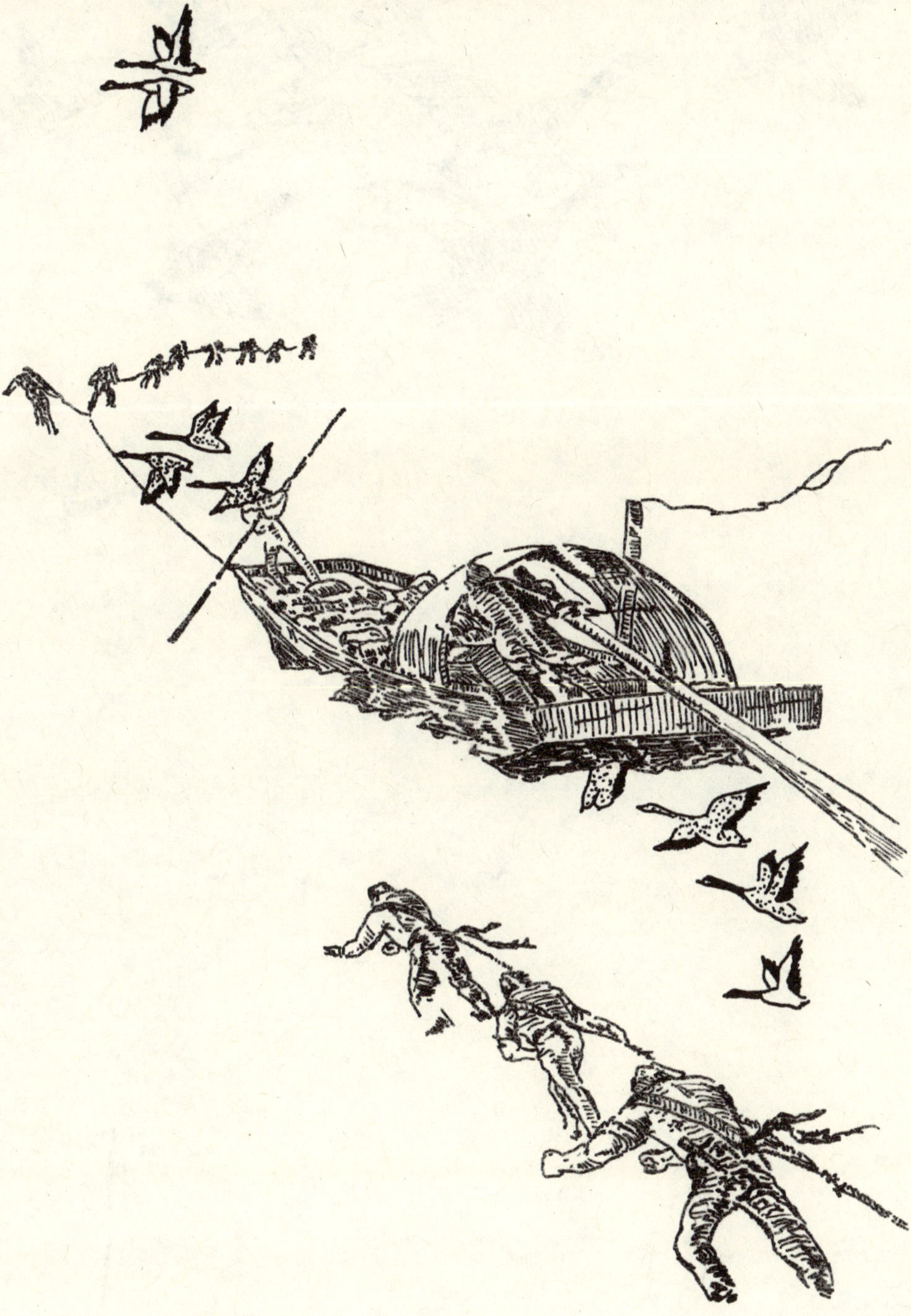

Grey wavering wedges

disciplined wedges

marshalled grey

Grey
grey

Clear cut grey
Dim
Stark

gray

grey

marshalled grey

marshalled gray
grey

gray

gray-winged, marshalled
marshalled

grey
wavering wedges

gray

Grey gray grey

through the mists against the rising sun
of the autumn
from
gales
autumn storms
from lowering sky

to
freedom and safety
toward the south
from the blue

through morning mists to distant
toward the south
feeding grounds
from lowering skies
from the sky
through snow and sleet
and darkness against pale tinted saffron dawn
over the
valley wide
against star strewn highways of the sky
on the
bars against golden radiance of the sun
to the south

on tireless wing
To friendly safety of their northern home
across the northern wilderness
of the verdant Spring

thro morning mists
over teeming, hostile haunts of men
on the bars
over friendly solemn solitudes
Above the trackless moor and reeking fen
from [illegible] star-filled
sky
O'er rolling woodlands where deep shadows lie
Above the foaming flood and nameless lake
With strident clamour of triumphant cry
from the star-filled skies
Above the harsh clamor of sound in man-made canyons below

on
sandy bar and in sanctuary of quiet reed bed
in the shadowy vale
On lonely hill along the wind swept shore
for the long
against an evening sky
flight from the friendly shelter of the north
As myriad voices tell their age-old tale
above the black lagoon
under the summer moon

over northern wilds
from the skies

out of the far-away South

through the mists against the rising sun

strident clangor

calling faintly

clamor of many voices
calling

honking

gabbling

clangor of many voices

honking

gabbling

call
clangor of many voices
*triumphant clarion*strident voice

triumphant

cry

Clamour strident clamour of triumphant cry

Gabbling

muted music

soft whir

whirr
call of wings a-drumming

triumphant clarion calls
call

wild free harmony

honking clangor

glad triumphant calls
call down a faint farewell

winging wing
winging fleeing

flying winging
calling passed

winging sent flying
passed honking calling
winging
sent flies
gabbling
fly gone

a-winging flew honking
come *come* *come*
gabbling filled
flying
Send

flies
wing*call*

Gabbling

marshalling
a-homing
homing homtell
a-drumming
driving sent
flew
winging honking
wavering sent *call*
flew
winging flew flies

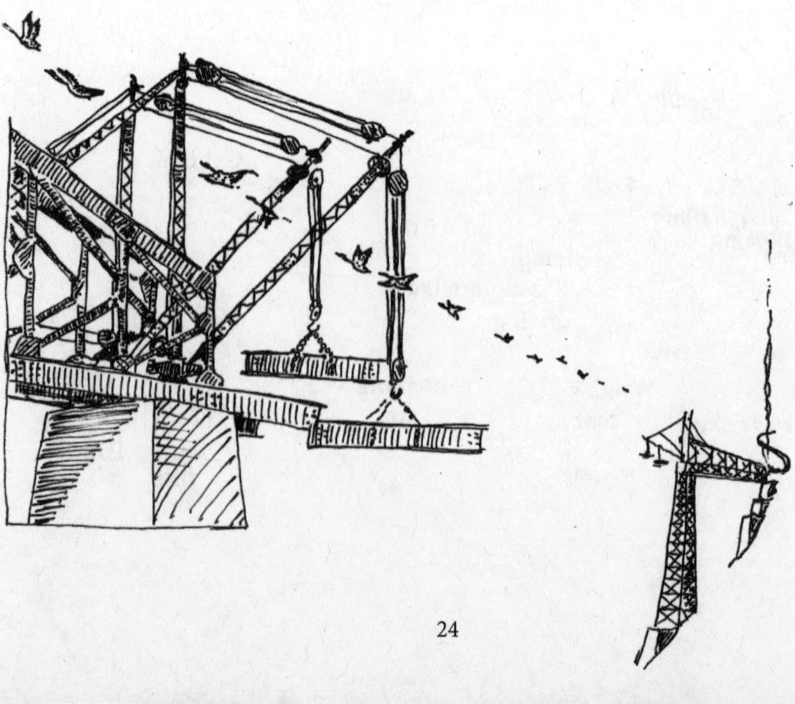

riders of the autumn

gales

disciplined wedges of sky-wanderers

marshalled hosts

sent down a last farewell

fancy

Stout-hearted heralds of the verdant Spring

winnowing *phant clarion cries from highways of the sky*

marshalled hosts

marshalled hosts

muted music

marshalling their companies and battalions

myriad voices

a-drumming

triumphant clarion calls wild free harmony

marshalled

hosts *My northland symphony!*

heavily southbound
faintly

reluctantlynorth

faintly

overhead

wearily

low

overhead

unfalteringly

down

high

North bound

overhead

High
Low
down

high

down

Wearily

south

late

tirelessly northward

down

out
down

down

winging wing weary way wavering wedges
wild winging

wedges Wild wanderers winging
way

whirring of wings
wild
wearily winging weary

wing
a-winging

Whirr of wings

winnowing wings

wild

Wearily wing

whir
waterfowl whirr waterfowl
wings

winging winged
wavering wedges of weary

winging

The Winnowing Wind

winging
wing
winging

winnowing wind *winnowing wind*
winging

winnowing wind *winnowing wind*

wings

winging

winging
winnowing wind *winnowing wind of War*

wing

a-winging

winnowing wind *winnowing wind*
wings

winnowing wings

wind *winnowing wind*

wing

wings

winged
winging
winds winnowed

winds winnowing
winging winds of war

I am coming I'm weary I am coming

I see

I climb I lean
I ask

I'm weary I hit
I hear

I'm smoking my head

guide

me let me

I'm wondering my peaceful solitude

I know

I have followed my tree I'll lie

about me
I might be

I have matched my wits

I'm chewing
Bringing me I'll always hold

I'm weary
I have taken
I shiver

I sit
I have ravished

give me

lull me I know

I sit

I see my buckskinned feet

my tiny cabin
I hear
I hear

I've drunk I hunger

I learned

I've drunk
I hunger

I hear I see *I know* welcome me

my vesper

I'll take

calling me

My nothing symphony *calling me*
I have followed *calling me*

The writer

the writer

the writer The writer

the writer *the writer*

the writer

the writer *the writer*

the writer

the writer either the writer

or one or more of his close associates

one of the writer's white friends of the north *the writer*

the writer

■■■■ the writer *the writer and a crew of* ■■■■ *and*

the writer

the Author

the writer

The writer *the writer*

Ells
Ells
S.C.E.
E.
Ells
Ells
S.C.E.
Ells
Ells
Ells
Ells
Ells
J.C.E.
Ells
Ells
Ells
Ells.
Ells.
Ells
Ells.
Ells
Ells
Ells.
Ells
Ells.
Ells
J.C.E.
Ells
Ells
Ells
Ells.
Ells.
Ells
Ells
Ells
S.C.E.
Ells
Ells.
Ells
Ells
J.C.E.
J.C.E
J.C. Ells.
Ells.
Ells
Ells
Ells
Ells
Ells

I I I
My
I

I I
I

I I my I
I my

me *My* me
my

I my
my
I

I my I
I me
I I my
me I
I I I

I I

me
me I
I
I my

I I *my*
I I
I I
I *I*
I I *I* me

I I me
My I *I* me *me*
me

S.C.Ells.

— S.C.E.

—S.C.E.

SCE

S.C.ELLS

S.C.E.

S.C.E.

S.C.E.

S.C.Ells

S.C.E.

S.C.E.

S.C.E.

S.C.Ells.

S.C.ELLS.

S.C.E.

S.C. Ells.

*bituminous sand**

bituminous sand

bitumen

bitumi-

nous sand

*Also referred to as "tar sand" and "oil sand".

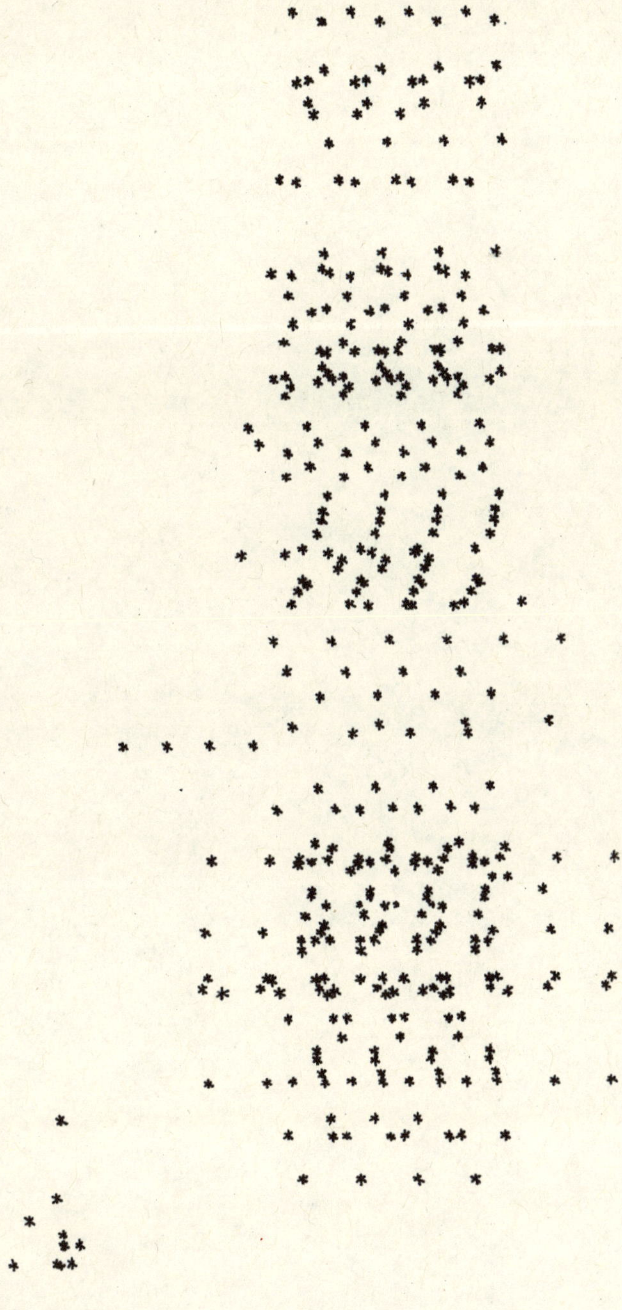

the tracking line(s)

М.Б.

The Athabaska Trail (1913)

Prior to the advent of the internal combustion engine along northern rivers, south-bound cargoes of furs were "tracked" upstream by brigades of large canoes and heavy bateaux—sometimes for many hundreds of miles. Crews of men harnessed to heavy "tracking" lines, hundreds of feet in length, fought their way grimly along the shores, often through tangle of overhanging brush, knee deep mud and waist deep water. The ceaseless torture of myriads of flies from daylight till dark, the harassing and heavy work which only the strongest men could long endure, made "tracking" one of the most brutal forms of labor.

In the late fall of 1913, the writer and a crew of ▬▬ and ▬▬ tracked the first important shipment of samples of bituminous sand[1] from McMurray up the rapids and fast water of Athabaska river to Athabaska Landing, a distance of nearly 250 miles. For twenty-three days, from daylight till dark, in snow and rain, the heavily loaded scow was hauled upstream. The following lines reflect, in part, the mental reaction,—a longing for rest—and warmth—and shelter.

[1]Ten tons.

"For twenty-three days through snow and rain . . ."

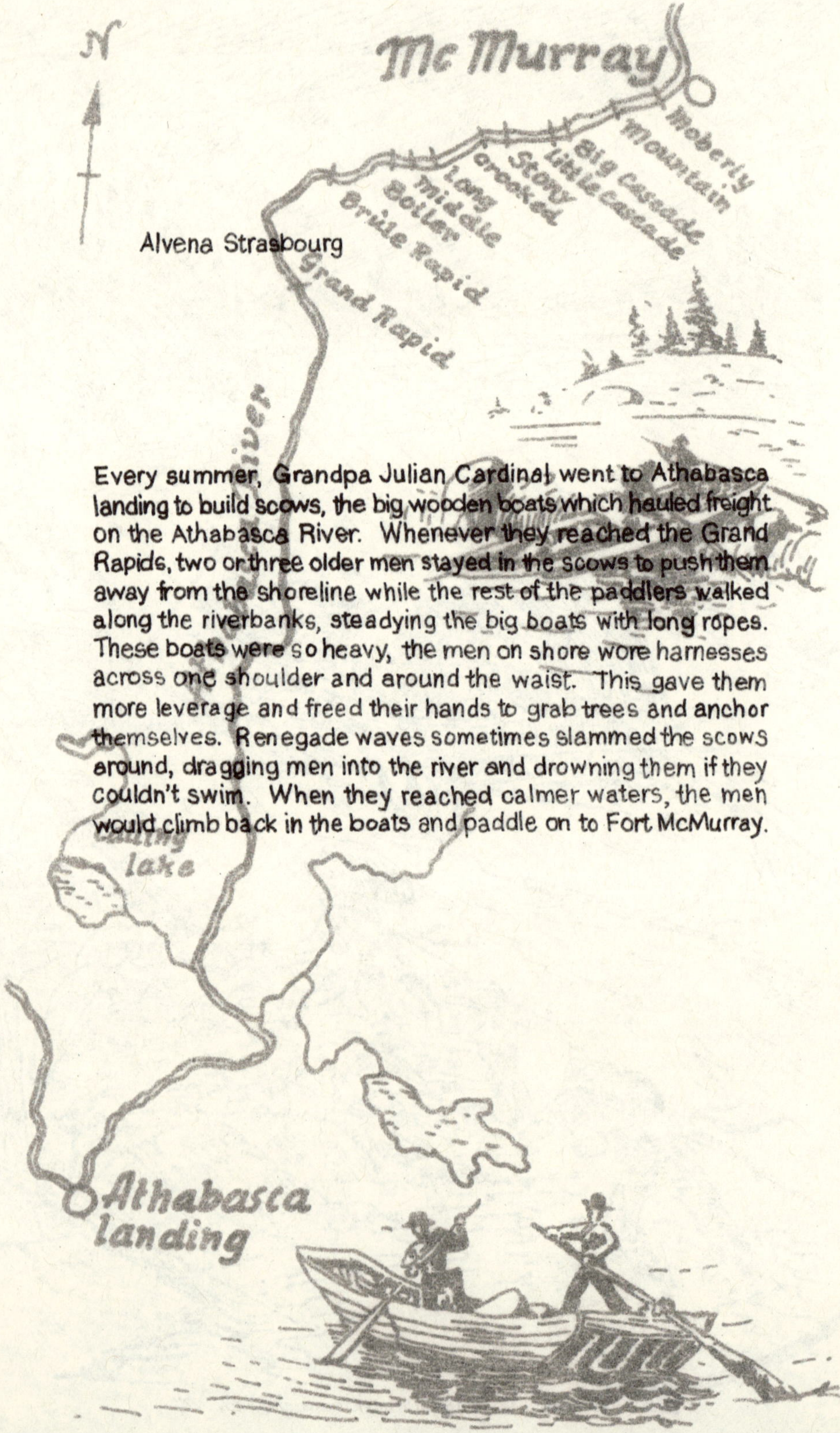

Alvena Strasbourg

Every summer, Grandpa Julian Cardinal went to Athabasca landing to build scows, the big wooden boats which hauled freight on the Athabasca River. Whenever they reached the Grand Rapids, two or three older men stayed in the scows to push them away from the shoreline while the rest of the paddlers walked along the riverbanks, steadying the big boats with long ropes. These boats were so heavy, the men on shore wore harnesses across one shoulder and around the waist. This gave them more leverage and freed their hands to grab trees and anchor themselves. Renegade waves sometimes slammed the scows around, dragging men into the river and drowning them if they couldn't swim. When they reached calmer waters, the men would climb back in the boats and paddle on to Fort McMurray.

And when we would go to town by boat, some of them they got no kicker. They have to paddle. Up stream. Some of them they pulled it with a rope, they tied it in the boat and pulled it like this and pulled it with a rope. Pull it like this, from the shore. That's the way they would do it. Well, people had a hard time. That's a long time ago. [laughs] Those are the stories I give you. Yeah, it wasn't very easy. Well, you can't make it one day like this, if you paddle from here. Swift water, really swift water. No, you couldn't make it in one day. Well, people would stop any place where it's nice to camp, they stop there. That's the way it happened.

ALICE BOUCHER

REPORT OF SUPERINTENDENT McDONELL.

SESSIONAL PAPER No. 28

Mr. T. C. Ellis, of the Department of Mines, passed through here en route to Ottawa in September with a quantity of both asphalt and oil sands to be tested in Ottawa.

first important shipment

good

ample

November 4th.,
(1913)

My dear Corporal,

deeply I am not going to write a letter, but merely to let you know officially that

are

young 'Bacon-face' and his associates
great
on the tracking line altogether worthy

best good

happy Yours very truly,

fitting Strong

I was wrong

November 4th.,
(1913)

My dear Corporal,

I I am

deeply regret

Oppressive

obnoxious As you are doubtless already aware,

astray

quite appalling, and

Yours very truly,

might find a watery grave, or come to some other fitting end.

somewhat twisted

It is

over not

a my

period intention

of to

streams, many emphasize

in years the

muskeg. timbered in difficulties

or a encountere

burned fly-

overinfested

areas, country,

and on

on many

almost

limitless

having

one secured

of and a

whom mysomewhat

spoke crew primitive

30-foot or of

scow understood three

English) white

men and

and my nine

an crew tons

(alleged) augmented of

by equipment

pilot a a

samples dozen

(only

line was laid out along the shore the tracking crew refused to move.

But when the 500-foot, 7/8-inch manilla tracking

At

this

critical

McMurray juncture

was (for

sioner) looking practically

leading La Nauze, on) the

harness RCMP, Constable entire

their on rushed (afterwards population

the own the down Assistant of

scow tongue. tracking the Commis-

gathered Thereupon line, river

headway. each and bank,

. man shouted seized

donned to the

his the

harnetsapkers

slowlyn

r g

r k

o a i h

i a

t i f

s t t

y l f

s r o a i

e a of u d

c d e l

e m

h u o l r

e e

d

s s t

s f

l r n

T e m y

of overhanging brush through a tangle

Harnessed

grimly to

along the

heavy

tracking

or waist deep in water

line,

men

fought

their

way

strewn

the rough

often ankle deep in mud beaches

boulder-

or

Breakfast was eaten by firelight;

we pulled on the line

until

dark

and then,

lacking tents,

slept under

the dripping trees.

hernia,

by the

either on

incapacitated"sick bay"

were the

men in

three placed

period and

this pneumonia

during or

appendicitis,

bottom of the leaky scow.

line Thereafter I took a place on the tracking

On three

occasions

during the

the journey

my " colleagues"

dropped their

their tracking harnesses

,

threw their blankets ashore

and

disappeared

into

the

bush

Patrol to Chipewyan

"Colleagues"

"deserters"

Oct. 13th Monday. Snowing & blowing all day & night. Passed Pt-Brule
[redacted] came and said he was 'starving' but refused a job on scow.

the missing trackers

RNWMP

Fortunately

they

had

21/7/13

not

Ft. McMurray

called

Alta

my

bluff!

*

snowed

seventeen

or

of

rained

the

throughout

twenty*three

* * * *

days.

had

Landing

*

Athabasca

at

It

lights scow. hours

of leaking * two

* * * *

glimmer and * and

faint battered McMurray*

the our leaving *

sawbeached after *

we we days *

darkEwenty-three *

*
afteznoon
*
and
*

*

*

*

*

and

withthatt

furthey r

findemuneration.

their

way

back

to

McMurray My salary at the time was $1800.

occupied

as

best time required it

the custom conditions they

established labour of

could

1913, regardless day

and

as the present-

late with

comparison as far

that, $45

purposted paid

For be be

maytrackers

that

It was

they also

in be an

a provided immutable

gunny with custom

sack moccasins that

full and

of tobacco the

each and for

at I me

a remunehad

Ottawa cost of to therefore

(The — — dirty swine.

reaching tobacdeclined $38.00. gratefuld

on Govanmment and

However, mocthesins indulgent

the of an

Depaofment

cost

(It

that may

the be

tobacco noted

consisted

of

plugs

which

were

rather

badly

mildewed).

)

campfires

northern was

around which

discussed a trip

long

(

The Athabaska Trail (1916)

the North West Company the use
the Hudson's Bay Company
the use the Union the use

the navigation the frequently rough and shallow water the
Athabaska
the larger
size

the bow the stern

The Athabaska Trail (1913)

the 75 miles the total fall

the heaviest the Grand rapid the fall
the advent the internal combustion engine
the Atha-
baska the western or main channel

the somewhat narrow channel the east side
the island the shores
The ceaseless torture
the harassing and
heavy work The Athabaska route the strongest men
the completion the most brutal forms

the late fall the writer
the north
the first important shipment
the fabulously rich empire the early fur traders.
the rapids the mineral empire

the spirit
the heavily loaded scow The following lines
the mental reaction the north
the early voyageur the national Hall of
Fame

the Alberta and Great Waterways Railway

the trackers the track-lines
the mist
the northland
the past the men

The yellow leaves

the high bush berries
the low bush berries
the wild hay
The days

The Athabaska Trail

the leaves
the willows the river the days
the north-
the riverward the woodlands

the autumn days the wind
the trail the wealth
The morning air the northland the rising the sun
the tracker's trail the mist the men the river side

the north the endless spruce
the evening sky

The silver stems
the autumn rain the wind
the grey geese the year

the early morn
The tracking line
the long the dew
the
noonday sun
the last
the long silence day's work the winding shore

Gone coiled

long

gone

yellow

Yellow gold brown

high bush crimson

low bush done

Sodden yellow wild

gone

Athabaska

gone

Silent swift

gold

autumn numbered wide bottom raw

cold

morning cold chill

tracker's

silent endless

inky clear cut evening

adorned golden graceful

tall

silver

autumn raw cold

grey

chill early

tracking

Wet

noonday

done

down
down

clumsily

clumsily down

one by one

Drearily
Wearily

old

heavy

wearily

Drip drip   patter patter

Drip drip   patter patter

Drip drip   patter patter

Drip drip   patter patter

Contents.

during early days of the present century

In referring to what is popularly known as "Canada's Last Great North"

Preface.

In industry, science

It is unfortunate that with notable exceptions

In the following pages

during upwards of forty years

For many years and in many parts of Canada

frequently under conditions of real hardship It was a time

Like many other engineers

By way of contrast during more recent years

It is hoped that

In the majority of episodes to which reference is made

Incidentally

many times the writer has regretted

with the return to civilization

during an idle hour

during idle moments

In conclusion

from time to time

NO
Ells.

The North

far
ice-bound
Masterful, untamed broad
Primitive, grim, and naked, fresh
ancient
shadowy
timid
daring
generous
lonely
blazing
lean and hungry
star-spangled
leaping, ruddy
cheerful bright
mellowed
Old
Choking
wind-swept
Foam-laced
crested
nameless
chequered
spacious
tawdry
gaudy
smug
petty
syncopated
tedious
new
wind-swept
shadowy
honking
sad
empty
stormy

of

of

of

of

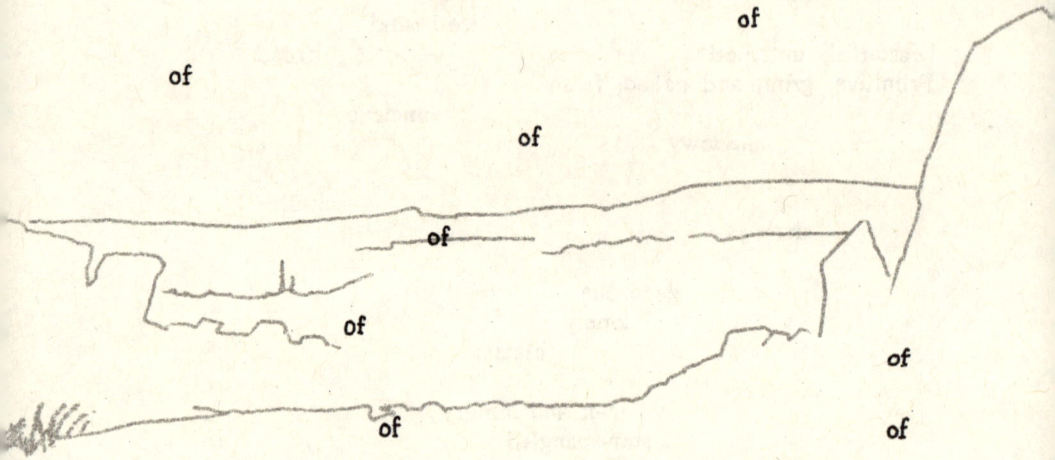

of

of

of

of

of

Canada's Barren

of of

of of

of

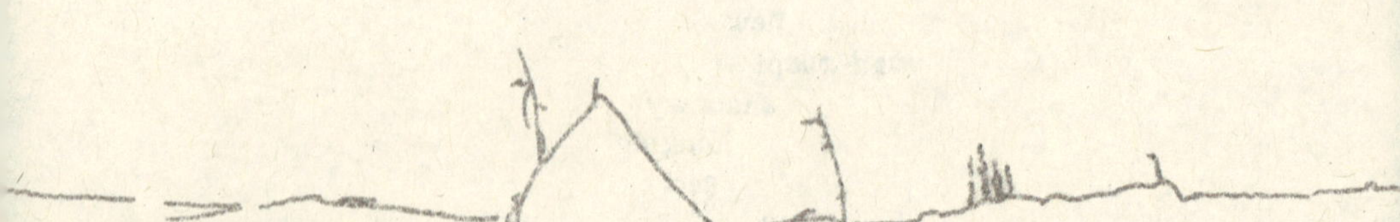

Canada's

thickets

spruce trees

forest

forest

mosses grasses

plants

rocks

scarps gullies

rocks

sandstone

streams rivers

forested

ponds lakes

water

minerals

land

The Seekers The Seekers

(Dedicated to the Canadian Prospector)

herdsman herdsman
husbandman husbandman
woodsman woodsman
sailorman sailorman

men men

Sons Sons men men

Sons Sons
Sons Sons
Men Men men men

Brothers Brothers
Brothers Brothers
Brothers Brothers
Brothers Brothers
Brothers Brothers
Brothers Brothers
Brothers Brothers men men

Men Men *men men*

Sires Sires sires sires
Sires Sires
Sires Sires
Sires Sires *men men* sires sires
Sires Sires sires sires
Sires Sires *men men*

brothers brothers
men men *sires sires men men*

My Lullaby

oo oo

oo

oo lu la

lu la

lu la oo oo

oo

oo oo

oo

oo

oo lu la

la lu

lu

oo oo la

la

lo

la

la

oo

oo oo

la

oo la oo

lu la

oo oo

oo

oo lu la

My Lullaby

oo oo
oo
oo lu la

lu la
lu la oo oo
oo

oo oo
oo
oo
oo lu la

la lu

lu

oo oo la
la

lo

la
la
oo
oo oo la

oo la oo
lu la

oo oo
oo

oo lu la

My Symphony.

h h o
n
h o n

h o n ho
h h o n
h o h o h o

H o n ho h o n

h o n k
h on
h h o
h o n k
h o n
h

h h h o
n h on ho
h o
n k
h o
h h on
h ho h
o h hon

Dad

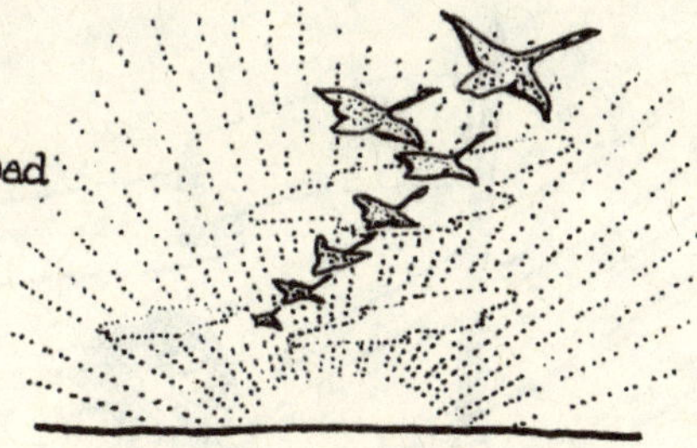

THE CALL!

Dad's Dad

Dad Tough as hickory known as Dad bruise

Dad's

hardy, aggressive and almost reckless

Dad

subdues the wilderness;

Dad

Dad

Dad's

soft whir

Dad's

primitive instincts

Dad's tiny fire

desire to live a natural life

Dad

desire

Dad Dad's

Dad

Dad's Dadly nature

• THE CHALLENGE •

The Challenge

great
dark
greatly daring smouldering
broadening
stern compelling
roaring
scorching flailing
dizzy
far
lowly glittering
rock-ribbed
trackless
shadowy
lofty
sullen mighty
nodding crannied
flaming bugle
human
breathless
trackless
new age-old
distant
new
lusty young bright
driving vagrant
drowsy babbling crested
gentle thudding
eerie lean grey sad wavering
myriad
empty Great

* * *

swinging northern midnight
verdant
inland Northland
Fair far grey

SILVER
FOX.
Ells.

"Towards the end of September Pelequin's canoe followed"

Toward the end of September, while blustering snow squalls dimmed crested hill and distant headland, Pelequin's canoe followed. Among the ragged willows and alders that fringed the shore, as best they could, followed the train dogs.

Twisting paddle, thrusting pole, straining tracking line! Sluggish backwaters, dappled with the woodland's tarnished gold, rushing streams flecked with gleaming foam, lonely lakes already fringed with young ice, slowly faded astern. Sweat-stained harness and galling packs! Heartbreaking portages that climbed steeply up and up over wet and slippery masses of rock, that wound their way through tangled mazes of fallen timber, that led from island to island across treacherous bog and slough, knee deep with stinking crusted slime—these had felt the tread of moccasined feet staggering under heavy loads; of burdened dogs tortured by cutting lashings of ill-adjusted packs. Yet night by night a ruddy camp-fire's wavering beacon moved ever farther north. Four weeks had passed ere Pelequin coiled his tracking line for the last time, stowed poles and paddles under the thwarts, and dragged his travel-scarred canoe—sole visible link with the great outer world—up the river bank through snow-encumbered bushes.

Now, cut off from the so-called comforts and amenities of civilization, dependent wholly on his own resourcefulness and strength, he must stand alone. Now he must summon to his aid the years of training in woodscraft and in the subtle art of trapping—if need be, day after day, must face undiscouraged, empty traps set with cunning skill. Now, for months to come, his companions were to be his dogs and his toboggan, his rifle, his axe, his traps. So far as he was concerned, kingdoms and states might crash, civilization itself collapse in bloody ruin, without causing a single ripple on the surface of his daily routine. Now, far from the nearest "Fort", the real business of life was to begin.

* * * *

"Heartbreaking portages that wound up and up over masses of rock."

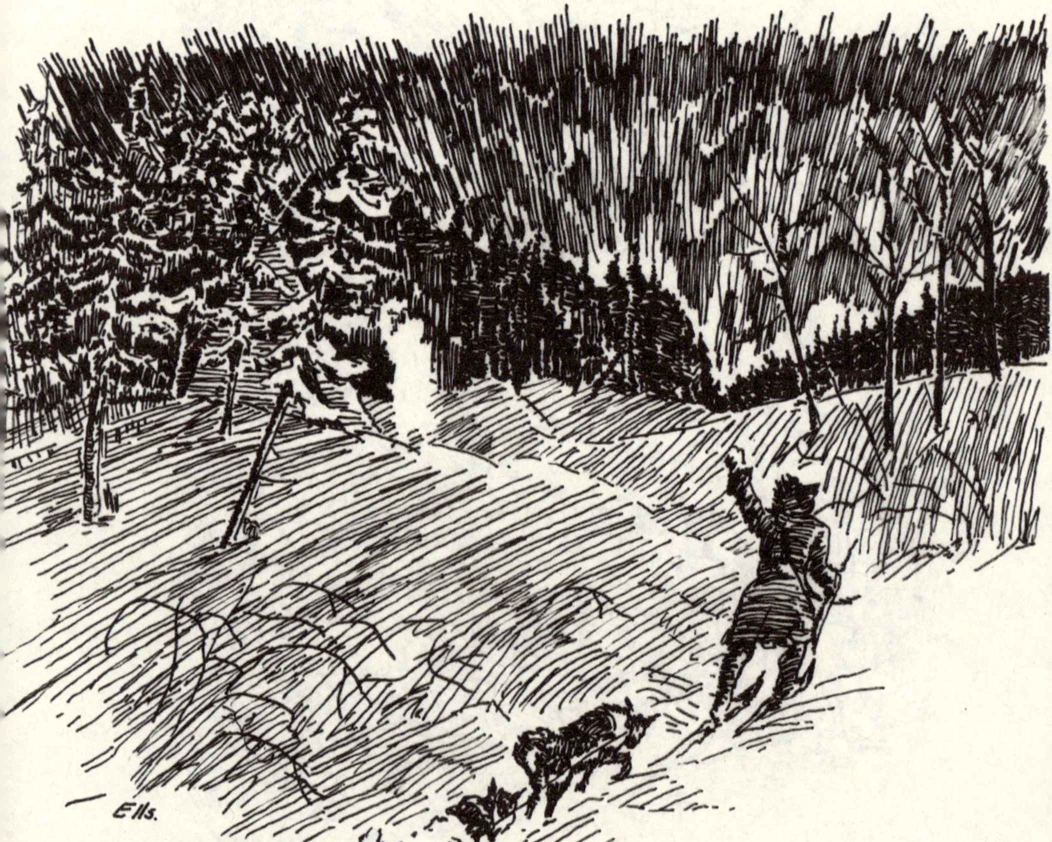

"In the friendly shelter of sturdy spruce stood Pelequin's teepee."

apart from Rose Marie,

I'm wearying

Farewell

I'm weary

I have followed

lands forlorn

I have matched a mother stern
mighty streams rolling down

I have taken

the morning air

I have ravished

the glittering skies

the solemn hush and peace of the North

and the treeless wastes

I have followed and trampled in welling blood winter's swirling calls!

EPILOGUE

not

let me lie

not alone   I'll lie

beneath my tree I'll lie   alone

alone

AFTERWORD

Sidney Clarke Ells (1878–1971) was a Canadian Department of Mines expert and World War I veteran whose work focused primarily on the Athabasca oil or tar sands from 1913 to 1945. For most of his career, Ells divided his time between Ottawa and Fort McMurray, Alberta, a former Hudson's Bay Company post and historic Métis community on Treaty 8 territory (Chipewyan, Cree, and Métis land). Known for his difficult personality and his stubborn determination to build an oil-sands industry for Canada, Ells liked to be called "the father of the tar sands." His early surveys, mining operations, and experiments with hot-water separation of bitumen from sand were foundational to the industry, but his legacy is often overshadowed by more-famous founders, especially University of Alberta expert Dr. Karl A. Clark, with whom Ells had a lifelong rivalry. The conflict was personal, and it also represented the struggle for control over the oil sands between the federal and provincial governments—a losing battle for Ells after mineral rights were transferred from Canada to Alberta in 1930. If the federal government's attempt to nationalize the tar sands with its Abasand project during World War II had been successful, Ells may have been remembered differently. Instead, when he retired in 1945, it was clear that the province would oversee the building of an oil-sands industry in northern Alberta, and that Clark would always be more celebrated than him. Ells lived to see the opening of the Great Canadian Oil Sands in 1967, but he did not attend the opening ceremonies.

I first heard about Ells and his mining work on a research trip to Fort McMurray in 2017, when I was early in the process of writing a thesis chapter on Canadian oil-worker poets that would eventually turn into a full dissertation and my scholarly book *The Rough Poets: Reading Oil-Worker Poetry*. Unfortunately, I didn't clue in that Ells was a poet until shortly after returning home, when I stumbled upon one of his poems in E. L. Chicanot's 1937 anthology *Rhymes of the Miner*. Ells was an amateur writer and artist, and throughout his career he made annual Christmas cards about the Athabasca region for friends and family; he also contributed illustrated poems, short stories, and essays to *Canadian Mining Journal* and *Canadian Geographical Journal*. Many of these works were collected and published by Garden City Press in 1938 as the book *Northland Trails*; a "new and enlarged edition" was published by Burns & MacEachern in 1956. Correspondence I found in Ells's papers suggests *Northland Trails* was a vanity publication. Despite this, the book seems to have been well-received. Ells saved clippings of twenty-six published reviews of his book, and the first library copy I ever read had once belonged to Canadian novelist Margaret Laurence.

Although *Northland Trails* often focuses on the labour of northern residents (fur-trade-era Indigenous and non-Indigenous labour as well as the modernizing labour of white prospectors and engineers), it makes few references to Ells's own work on the tar sands. I found this omission intriguing, and Ells soon became my thesis rabbit hole—the thing I researched and researched and then struggled to cram into one still-too-long chapter. I read everything I could about Ells, Fort McMurray, and early twentieth-century work on the oil sands. I travelled twice to Ottawa in 2018 to visit Ells's fonds at Library and Archives Canada, where I saw evidence that he spent his retirement obsessively revising his memoir and trying to maintain control of the narrative about who started it all. On one of those trips, I went to Beechwood Cemetery in Ottawa to visit his grave. I disliked Ells, and I sensed he would dislike me, yet I was also fascinated. While doing more traditional scholarly writing about Ells, I also began writing poems about him and experimenting with poetic ways to respond to *Northland Trails*.

Around this time, I served for three years as a co-editor of the Association for Literature, Environment, and Culture in Canada's hybrid scholarly and literary journal *The Goose*. Sometimes I would put on a goose persona to post on social media or to write calls for submissions. This involved a lot of honking and using fun words like *gaggle*. In my courses at the University of Winnipeg, I was teaching Kate Beaton's webcomics about working in the tar sands—early versions of her graphic novel *Ducks: Two Years in the Oil Sands* that link the lives of workers with the 2008 drowning of 1,600 ducks in a Syncrude tailings pond. At some point, a playful hypothesis occurred to me: there are lots of geese in *Northland Trails*, and I began to suspect that Ells, who migrated each year between Ottawa and Fort McMurray and who wanted to be seen as a legitimate resident of the north, may have liked to think of himself as a goose. While penning romantic poems describing the sounds of geese as "My Symphony," Ells could not have anticipated the irony that, decades later, it would be the deaths of so many waterfowl that would turn global and local public opinion against the industry he was so proud to have fathered. What he may have anticipated (although he certainly didn't admit it if he did) is that the industry would turn out to be infamously and irreparably destructive to his beloved northland. Inspired by books like Jordan Abel's *The Place of Scraps*, M. NourbeSe Philip's *Zong!*, Syd Zolf's *Janey's Arcadia*, Shane Rhodes's *Dead White Men*, and Lesley Battler's *Endangered Hydrocarbons*, I started to make visual poetry out of found text and images from *Northland Trails*. After some experimentation, I developed a method of building poems and critical arguments about *Northland Trails* by tracing words and illustrations from its pages.

When I first began working on these poems, the 1938 edition of *Northland Trails* was available and searchable online, so it was possible to do a quick search for every instance of a word like *goose*. In retrospect, it would have been more efficient to digitize the 1956 edition, which readers may be interested to know is now also available online. Instead, I made the poems by carefully reading the 1956 edition and marking instances of words and images I wanted to work with, then tracing them onto thin sheets of paper with very fine pens. With some exceptions, I worked with the constraint of tracing these elements exactly where they appear on Ells's pages, moving my poems from page to page and letting the markings overlap. Working in an unforgiving medium, where often the only way to fix a mistake or make a revision was to start over, and where a new idea for a poem usually meant reading or skimming *Northland Trails* again, I made multiple versions of each poem. For "the tracking line(s)," I did archival research on tracking scows on the Athabasca River—looking for either the names of the Métis and First Nations trackers Ells hired in 1913 or any Indigenous accounts of what it was like to do this work. I didn't find much of what I was looking for—this is something I hope to continue to research. In 2023, 110 years after the journey Ells writes about in his poem "The Athabaska Trail," I took a carbon-intensive trip to retrace the route he and the trackers travelled along the Athabasca River from Fort McMurray to Athabasca, including scrambling over the boulder-strewn shores of the Grand Rapids that they also scrambled over while towing a boat upstream. In "the tracking line(s)," I contextualize "The Athabaska Trail" by drawing on outside historical and archival sources, including text from Ells's memoir, which I traced while shifting the pages to imitate the movement of the river and the steps and stumbles of the trackers.

Goose is a work of research-creation that blends research, literary criticism, and poetics. My tracing method pulls at and draws out threads of ideology, power, subversion, and contradiction in *Northland Trails*, sidelining its more overt or obvious content to pay attention to its underlying assumptions and aesthetics, along with the things it tries to hide or contain. *Goose* interprets *Northland Trails* by following a succession of clues, hunches, and ideas, driven not by the need to prove that they are correct but rather to ask, only ever half seriously, what if they were? Looking for geese in *Northland Trails* leads to looking for dissenting perspectives and voices more generally. It loosens Ells's grip on geese as metaphor or pathetic fallacy, creating space for geese—along with other northern beings, including Indigenous peoples, non-human animals, and the land itself—to exist beyond and in resistance to the uses Ells puts them to. As a deconstructive project working on and against settler-colonial ideology, *Goose* seeks, holds space for, and invites readers to investigate Indigenous and decolonial counternarratives to *Northland Trails*.

As Ells neared the end of his life and watched the tar-sands industry he had dreamed of come into being, he liked to boast that he had started and foreseen it all. Today, in the time of climate emergency, pollution, and the open questions of when the oil-sands project will finally be put to rest and who will take responsibility to clean up the lands and waters it has destroyed, I wonder why anyone would want to be called the father of the tar sands. *Goose* investigates colonial, racist, and sexist logics and aesthetics that are foundational to extractive industry and the Canadian nation-state. It celebrates dissenters—the trackers, and others like Métis Elder and Indigenous employment advocate Alvena Strasbourg—as true visionaries who have resisted, challenged, and held industry and government accountable since the beginning. While Alberta and Canada continue to subsidize and defend the oil-sands industry, pretending it is ethical or practical to build fossil infrastructure while our communities sicken, flood, and burn, in *Goose* I speak with, to, and as Ells as a way of reckoning with my own inheritance and responsibilities as a settler citizen of a petrostate built on stolen land. It's time to give up the individualist, modernist narratives of an industry or a nation built against all odds by larger-than-life founding fathers. May we face the polycrisis with humility, cooperation, Indigenous leadership, and care for the land, one another, and future generations.

Melanie Dennis Unrau

NOTES

Page 5: S. C. Ells, *Northland Trails* (Toronto: Burns & MacEachern, 1956), public domain.

Pages 7–9: S. C. Ells, *Northland Trails* (Toronto: Garden City Press, 1938), public domain.

Pages 10–47: Ells, *Northland Trails*, 1956 ed.

Page 46: This poem is for Rina Garcia Chua.

Page 49: Ells, *Northland Trails*, 1956 ed.; S. C. Ells, *Recollections of the Development of the Athabasca Oil Sands* (Ottawa: Dept. of Mines and Technical Surveys, 1962), public domain.

Page 51: "Getting asphalt from Fort McMurray tar sands, Alberta," 1914, (CU1154016) by Unknown. Courtesy of Glenbow Library and Archives Collection, Libraries and Cultural Resources Digital Collections, University of Calgary, public domain. Description in archival record: "First shipment. Taken on scow that was tracked up the Athabasca River for 240 miles. Sidney Ells and party hauled the barge." I believe Ells took this photo in 1913.

Pages 52–53: Ells, *Northland Trails*, 1956 ed.

Page 54: Alvena Strasbourg, *Memories of a Metis Woman: Fort McMurray Yesterday & Today* (self-published, 1998), 8, used with permission; Robert Kunz, map illustrating "The Last of the Brigades" by Guy Blanchet, *Northern Treasury: Selections from The Beaver*, ed. Clifford Wilson (Toronto: Thomas Nelson & Sons, 1955), 74, public domain.

Page 55: Alice Boucher, in Craig Campbell, Alice Boucher, Mike Evans, Emma Faichney, Howard LaCorde, and Zachary Powder, *mihkwâkamiwi sîpîsis: Stories and Pictures from Metis Elders in Fort McKay* (Edmonton: Canadian Circumpolar Institute, 2005), 14, used with permission (Elder Alice Boucher's story appears alongside the same 1913 photograph of trackers that is on page 51 of *Goose*); "Annual Report of Superintendent A.E.C. McDonell, Commanding 'N' Division, Athabaska Landing," *Report of the Royal Northwest Mounted Police 1913* (Ottawa: C.H. Parmelee, 1913), 133, public domain; Ells, *Northland Trails*, 1956 ed.

Pages 56–57: S. C. Ells, Letter to Corporal Lanauze [sic], 4 Nov. 1913. Library and Archives Canada, Ottawa, Sidney Clarke Ells fonds, R4495-0-7-E, vol. 1, public domain.

Page 58: S. C. Ells, "Loading Bituminous Sand at Murphy Claim, Athabasca River, Alta," 1913, Canada. Dept. of Mines and Technical Surveys, Library and Archives Canada, PA-013556, public domain.

Pages 59–66: Ells, *Recollections*.

Page 67: Ells, *Recollections*; Charles "Denny" La Nauze, Diary + notebook, 1912–1914. Glenbow Library and Archives Collection, University of Calgary, Denny La Nauze fonds, M-9581-1, public domain.

Pages 68–69: Ells, *Recollections.*

Page 70: Ells, *Recollections*, 13; Ells's added annotations on a copy of his *Recollections*, n.d., Library and Archives Canada, Ottawa, Sidney Clarke Ells fonds, R4495-0-7-E, vol. 12, public domain.

Pages 71–72: Ells, *Recollections.*

Page 73: S. C. Ells, "Tracking, Athabasca R., Alta," 1923, Canada. Dept. of Mines and Technical Surveys, Library and Archives Canada, PA-013609, public domain. I believe Ells took this photo in 1913.

Pages 74–105: Ells, *Northland Trails*, 1956 ed.

ACKNOWLEDGEMENTS

I respectfully acknowledge the original caretakers of the land known as Treaty 1 territory/Winnipeg, where I live as a settler of mixed European ancestry on the traditional territory of the Anishinaabeg, Ininiwak, Anishininewuk, Dakota Oyate, and Dene peoples and the homeland of the Red River Métis.

Early versions of these poems were published in a chapbook titled *The Goose* (above/ground press, 2022); in a zine titled *the tracking lines* (DIY Methods, 2023); in *Mosaic: An Interdisciplinary Critical Journal* 55, no. 2 (2022): 149–65; in *Banff 2023 Winter Writers Residency: The Antholozine*, edited by Kate Siklosi and Dani Spinosa (2023); in rob mclennan's "Spotlight Series #65" on *Medium* (2021); as a broadside for knife|fork|book Fertile Festival by Gap Riot Press (2022); as an off-site (virtual) reading for rob mclennan's blog (2023); and on the Chaudiere Books blog (2024). Thanks to these incredible publishers and colleagues for their support.

Many thanks to Leigh, Andrew, and Debby at Assembly Press for getting what I was trying to do with *Goose* and for your enthusiasm and support to make it into a book. Thanks to my editor, Jordan Abel, for helping me shape this collection and consider its ethics. Thanks to McMurray Métis Local 1935, especially Bryan Fayant, for hosting me as a guest in early 2025, and to Elders Frank LaCaille, Leonard Hansen, and Harvey Sykes for an enlightening conversation about work on the Athabasca River and its significance. I'm deeply grateful to Tim Clark and McMurray Métis for providing a foreword for this book.

Thanks to the many people who have workshopped, worked alongside, read, and supported this project, including Warren Cariou, Emily Eaton, Michael Trussler, Isabella Huberman, Kaie Kellough, Kate Siklosi, Dani Spinosa, Yvette Cenerini, Troni Grande, Kathleen Wall, Medrie Purdham, Jes Battis, Tracy Hamon, Tara Dawn Solheim, Samantha F. Jones, Mike Gismondi, Lori Claerhout, Rina Garcia Chua, Alec Follett, Hee-Jung Serenity Joo, Ekene Emeka-Maduka, Shep Steiner, Jocelyn Thorpe, Sanita Fejzić, Joanna Lilley, Ariel Gordon, Yvonne Blomer, Sarah Deckert, Jason Unrau, Courtney Unrau, Sheldon Unrau, and my fellow participants at two pivotal virtual writing residencies at the Banff Centre for the Arts. Thanks also to the archivists, librarians, researchers, copyright advisers, and even helicopter pilots who supported my research. I'm grateful to Darcy, Shirley, and Shelley of Grand Rapids Wilderness Adventures for an unforgettable visit to the Grand Rapids and trip along the Athabasca River with Emily Eaton in 2023. To my former colleagues at *The Goose*: the warmest and friendliest *HONK*.

I wish to acknowledge and thank the Banff Centre for Arts and Creativity, the Social Sciences and Humanities Research Council of Canada for the two post-doctoral fellowships I held while producing these poems, the Faculty of Arts and Research Office at the University of Regina for research funding, and the University of Manitoba Institute for the Humanities, St. John's College at the University of Manitoba, and the Humanities Research Institute at the University of Regina for research and visiting fellowships.

To my family, friends, neighbours, and community—deep gratitude and love.

Photo credit: Jason Unrau

Melanie Dennis Unrau is a poet, editor, scholar, and climate organizer of mixed European ancestry from Winnipeg, Manitoba, traditional territory of the Anishinaabeg, Ininiwak, Anishininewuk, Dakota Oyate, and Dene peoples and the homeland of the Red River Métis. She is the author of the literary study *The Rough Poets: Reading Oil-Worker Poetry* (McGill-Queen's UP, 2024) and the poetry collection *Happiness Threads: The Unborn Poems* (The Muses' Company, 2013). A former editor of *The Goose* journal and *Geez* magazine, Melanie also co-edited *I'll Get Right On It: Poems on Working Life in the Climate Crisis* (Roseway, 2025).

RECYCLED
Paper
FSC® C100212

Printed by Imprimerie Gauvin
Gatineau, Québec